The Story of a Special Day
Volume 163

June
11

The 162ᵗʰ day of the year (163ʳᵈ in leap years). There are 203 days remaining until the end of the year.

by Michael Dobson

Timespinner
Press

This book is also available in e-book form for Kindle, e-pub devices, and other formats from your favorite online booksellers.

For more information about the series, about us, or about your special day, please email us at editor@timespinnerpress.com.

Look for other volumes in *The Story of a Special Day*, coming often. See www.timespinnerpress.com for details and for the most recent information.

Table of Contents

Cover: *Declaration of Independence*, by John Trumbull (1819) The "Committee of Five" was appointed to begin writing the declaration on June 11, 1776 — the **EVENT OF THE DAY**. (Courtesy Architect of the Capitol) The painting is also on the back of the US$2 bill.

Quote of the Day

"I made history and therefore did not find
time to write it."

Klemens von Metternich
diplomat and statesman, died June 11 , 1859

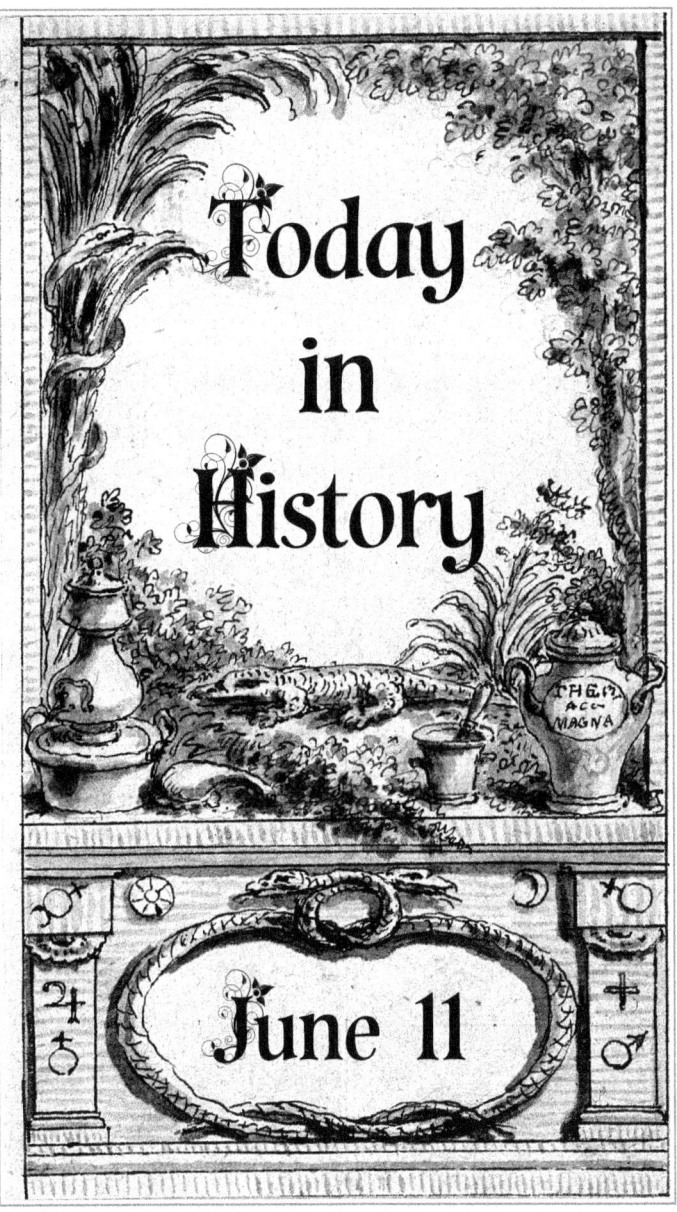

Today in History

June 11

Detail from the cover painting *Declaration of Independence*, by John Trumbull. From left to right: John Adams, Roger Sherman, Robert Livingston, Thomas Jefferson, and Benjamin Franklin

Event of the Day
The Declaration of Independence

On June 11, 1776, the US Second Continental Congress appointed the Committee of Five to draft and present a proposed Declaration of Independence for the thirteen colonies.

The five members, in alphabetical order, were John Adams (later the second US president), Benjamin Franklin (then US minister to France, later postmaster general), Thomas Jefferson (later the third US president), Robert Livingston (later negotiated the Louisiana Purchase), and Roger Sherman (the only man to sign all four of the founding documents of the United States.)

Although the original Thirteen Colonies that made up British North America were nominally independent of one another, it was increasingly clear that their mutual interests were entwined.

In 1774, in response to the "Intolerable Acts" passed by the British government following the Boston Tea Party, representatives of twelve of the colonies met in Philadelphia in what became known as the First Continental Congress. At the time, they decided not to declare independence, settling instead for a petition to King George III — which was not well received.

The Intolerable Acts created great resentment in Massachusetts especially, because they were designed to punish those involved in the Boston Tea Party.

When local militias began to organize, the British government declared Massachusetts to be in a state of rebellion, and sent a force of 700 British soldiers to capture their supplies and quell the rebellion. However, the rebels learned of the advancing British forces, and Paul Revere (among others) rode to alert the rebels.

The result was the opening battle in the American Revolutionary War, the Battles of Lexington and Concord. The British were driven back to Boston.

With war inevitable, a Second Continental Congress was called in the summer of 1775 to take charge of the war effort. The rag-tag militias were organized into the Continental Army, and delegate George Washington of Virginia was appointing commanding general.

Although the Congress made one final attempt (the Olive Branch Petition) to avoid the conflict, the petition reached Britain too late to do any good. Although at the time there was no official "United States of America" to govern, the Second Continental Congress took on the duties of a national government for the duration of the war, issuing money, signing treaties, and appointing ambassadors.

There was still no final decision about American

independence. Many delegates still hoped to avoid such a drastic action and hoped that peaceful terms could still be achieved. Slowly, however, the sentiment for a separation from Great Britain won the day.

On June 7, 1776, Richard Henry Lee of Virginia offered a resolution to declare the colonies independent. In response, the Continental Congress created three committees: one to write a Declaration of Independence, one to develop a Model Treaty for foreign relations, and one to develop Articles of Confederation to provide a legal framework for the new country.

The Committee of Five, established on June 11, had three weeks to develop a formal declaration of American independence. They first agreed on a general outline, then assigned one of their number, Thomas Jefferson, to prepare a first draft.

A draft portion of the Declaration of Independence. The handwritten changes are by Benjamin Franklin (Courtesy Library of Congress)

Writing the Declaration of Independence, Jean Leon Gerome Ferris

It took Jefferson 17 days to create that initial draft. The other four members reviewed the draft and made extensive changes, and on Friday, June 28, 1776, the Committee presented the final version to the entire Congress. The debate took place the following Monday, July 1, and on July 2, 1776, the Second Continental Congress, by unanimous vote, officially declared the independence of the United States of America.

This notable event caused future president John Adams to write, "The second day of July, 1776, will be the most memorable epocha in the history of America. I am apt to believe that it will be celebrated by succeeding generations as the great anniversary festival."

Of course, American Independence Day is celebrated on July 4, not July 2. Although the actual declaration of independence was passed on July 2, the members of Congress debated the text of the declaration until the next day, removing a denunciation of slavery among other changes, finally finishing debate at the end of the July 3 session.

The vote on the text of the Declaration of Independence took place the morning of July 4, and thus the opening line of the Declaration of Independence reads, "In Congress, July 4, 1776, The unanimous Declaration of the thirteen united State of America." leading to the general belief that American independence began July 4, not July 2.

Not all the people who signed the Declaration of Independence did so immediately. It wasn't until July 5 that a clean final copy was available, and most of the signing took place on August 2. One person didn't sign until November 4.

Regardless of the date of drafting or the date of signing, the Declaration of Independence has become one of the most famous documents, not merely in American history, but also worldwide. Other declarations of independence have used the American declaration as an inspiration, and many have even taken many sections directly from the document.

Its opening sentence, "We hold these truths to be self-evident, that all men are created equal, that they are endowed by their Creator with certain unalienable Rights, that among these are Life, Liberty, and the pursuit of Happiness," has been called "one of the best known sentences in the English language." Although this guiding principle hasn't always been followed, it is generally considered to be the moral standard to which the United States should strive. Abraham LIncoln considered it to be the foundation of his political philosophy.

The Committee of Five consisted of some of the finest minds in America, and its impact not only affects Americans, but every citizen in the world who strives for freedom.

(335)

The PENNSYLVANIA EVENING POST.

Price only Two Coppers. Published every *Tuesday, Thursday,* and *Saturday* Evenings.

Vol. II.]   SATURDAY, JULY 6, 1776.   [Num. 228.

In CONGRESS, July 4, 1776.
A Declaration by the Representatives of the United States of America, in General Congress assembled.

WHEN, in the course of human events, it becomes necessary for one people to dissolve the political bands which have connected them with another, and to assume, among the powers of the earth, the separate and equal station to which the laws of nature and of nature's God intitle them, a decent respect to the opinions of mankind requires that they should declare the causes which impel them to the separation.

We hold these truths to be self-evident, That all men are created equal, that they are endowed, by their Creator, with certain unalienable rights ; that among these are life, liberty, and the pursuit of happiness. That to secure these rights, governments are instituted among men, deriving their just powers from the consent of the governed ; that whenever any form of government becomes destructive of these ends, it is the right of the people to alter or to abolish it, and to institute new government, laying its foundation on such principles, and organizing its powers in such form, as to them shall seem most likely to effect their safety and happiness. Prudence, indeed, will dictate that governments long established should not be changed for light and transient causes ; and accordingly all experience hath shewn, that mankind are more disposed to suffer, while evils are sufferable, than to right themselves by abolishing the forms to which they are accustomed. But when a long train of abuses and usurpations, pursuing invariably the same object, evinces a design to reduce them under absolute despotism, it is their right, it is their duty, to throw off such government, and to provide new guards for their future security. Such has been the patient sufferance of these colonies, and such is now the necessity which constrains them to alter their former systems of government. The history of the present King of Great-Britain is a history of repeated injuries and usurpations, all having in direct object the establishment of an absolute tyranny over these states. To prove this, let facts be submitted to a candid world.

He has refused his assent to laws, the most wholesome and necessary for the public good.

He has forbidden his Governors to pass laws of immediate and pressing importance, unless suspended in their operation till his assent should be obtained ; and, when so suspended, he has utterly neglected to attend to them.

He has refused to pass other laws for the accommodation of large districts of people, unless those people would relinquish the right of representation in the legislature, a right inestimable to them, and formidable to tyrants only.

He has called together legislative bodies at places unusual, uncomfortable, and distant from the depository of their public records, for the sole purpose of fatiguing them into compliance with his measures.

He has dissolved Representative Houses repeatedly, for opposing with manly firmness his invasions on the rights of the people.

He has refused for a long time, after such dissolutions, to cause others to be elected ; whereby the legislative powers, incapable of annihilation, have returned to the people at large for their exercise ; the state remaining in the mean time exposed to all the dangers of invasion from without, and convulsions within.

He has endeavoured to prevent the population of these states ; for that purpose obstructing the laws for naturalization of foreigners ; refusing to pass others to encourage their migrations hither, and raising the conditions of new appropriations of lands.

He has obstructed the administration of justice, by refusing his assent to laws for establishing judiciary powers.

He has made Judges dependant on his will alone, for the tenure of their offices, and the amount and payment of their salaries.

He has erected a multitude of new offices, and sent hither swarms of officers to harrass our people, and eat out their substance.

He has kept among us, in times of peace, standing armies, without the consent of our legislatures.

He has affected to render the military independant of and superior to the civil power.

He has combined with others to subject us to a jurisdiction foreign to our constitution, and unacknowledged by our laws ; giving his assent to their acts of pretended legislation :

For quartering large bodies of armed troops among us :

For protecting them, by a mock trial, from punishment for any murders which they should commit on the inhabitants of these states :

For cutting off our trade with all parts of the world :

For imposing taxes on us without our consent :

For depriving us, in many cases, of the benefits of trial by jury :

For transporting us beyond seas to be tried for pretended offences :

For abolishing the free system of English laws in a neighbouring province, establishing therein an arbitrary government, and enlarging its boundaries, so as to render it at once an example and fit instrument for introducing the same absolute rule into these colonies :

For taking away our charters, abolishing our most valuable laws, and altering fundamentally the forms of our governments :

For suspending our own legislatures, and declaring themselves invested with power to legislate for us in all cases whatsoever.

He has abdicated government here, by declaring us out of his protection and waging war against us.

He has plundered our seas, ravaged our coasts, burnt our towns, and destroyed the lives of our people.

He is, at this time, transporting large armies of foreign mercenaries to complete the works of death, desolation, and tyranny, already begun with circumstances of cruelty and

The first newspaper publication of the Declaration of Independence, Pennsylvania Evening Post, July 6, 1776.

Jeanne d'Arc blessée à la bataille de Jargeau (Joan of Arc wounded at the battle of Jargeau), Jargeau, Loriet, France

What Happened on June 11?

From the creation of great works of engineering and art, to devastating wars and natural disasters, thousands of years of history have left their mark on each and every day of the year. Here are some important events that occurred on June 11. (Illustrated items are boxed.)

1489 — **Joan of Arc leads her troops in her first offensive battle,** the Battle of Jargeau. It ends the following day with a French victory.

1509 — **Henry VIII of England marries Catherine of Aragon**, his first wife. She will reign as queen until 1533, when her marriage is annulled so that Henry VIII could marry Anne Boleyn.

1895 — **The first automobile race**, the Paris-Bordeaux-Paris Trail, begins. After 48 hours and nearly 1,200 kilometers, Émile Levassor reaches the finish line, but is disqualified because his car is a two-seater and the race was for four-seater cars. The eventual winner, Paul Koechlin, arrives exactly 11 hours later. *(Photo next page.)*

1919 — Racehorse Sir Barton wins the Belmont Stakes, becoming **the first horse ever to win the Triple Crown.**

1955 — In the **deadliest event in the history of motorsports,** the *24 Hours of Le Mans* race ends in a crash that flings large amounts of debris into the watching crowds, killing 83 spectators and one of the drivers and injuring 120 more.

1962 — In what may have been the **only successful escape from Alcatraz Prison,** three inmates place papier-mâché heads in their own likenesses into their beds to fool the guards, break out of the main prison, and leave the island on an improvised inflatable raft. Their fate remains unknown.

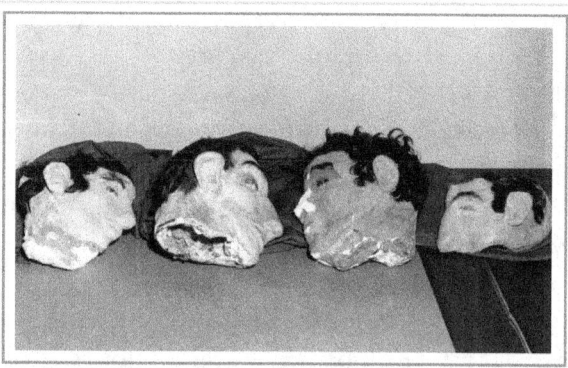

The dummy heads used in the 1962 escape from Alcatraz Prison
(Courtesy FBI)

1970 — The **first two women to become generals in the US armed forces,** Anna Mae Hays and Elizabeth Paschel Hoisington, receive their new rank.

1971 — The **Native American occupation of Alcatraz Island ends** after 19 months a large force of US officers removes the final 15 people from the island.

Émile Levassor and Charles d'Hostingue in the 1895 Paris-Bordeaux-Paris Trail race

Quote of the Day

"Sometimes we are lucky enough to know
that our lives have been changed, to
discard the old, embrace the new, and turn
headlong down an immutable course."

Jacques-Yves Cousteau, oceanographer and
filmmaker, inventor of the Aqualung
born June 11, 1910

Births
and
Deaths

THER.
ACT.
MAGNA

June 11

Film poster for the 1934 film *Blue Steel,* starring John Wayne.
John Wayne died June 11, 1979

Notable June 11 People

With the current world population at about seven billion people, on average about 19 million people also celebrate their birthdays on June 11 — and that isn't counting the millions and millions who came before! No matter when you were born, you share your birthday with many special people whose accomplishments (and occasionally embarrassments) have been noted as part of history.

In this section, you'll meet fascinating people who share your birthday. They're organized by what they're famous for, and then in reverse chronological order from most recent to earliest. Those who are shown in photographs or artwork have a box around them. We don't have photos of everyone, so please forgive us if your favorite person is missing.

Some of these people you've heard of, others may be new to you, but they all make up an important part of the reason that June 11 is a truly special day!

Dedham Vale, by John Constable

Who Was Born on June 11?

Art and Illustration

John Constable, painter known for his landscapes of the English Dedham Vale area, now known as "Constable Country." *(1776)*

Business

Marco Arment, computer entrepreneur who created Instapaper and co-founded Tumblr. *(1982)*

Kiichiro Toyoda (豊田 喜一郎), Japanese entrepreneur who took his father's loom works business and turned it into Toyota Motor Corporation, the largest automobile manufacturer in the world. *(1894)*

Crime and Punishment

Henry Hill, mobster who later became an FBI informant; his book *Wiseguy* formed the basis for the 1990 Martin Scorsese film *Goodfellas,* in which HIll was played by Ray Liotta. *(1943)*

Bartolomeo Vanzetti, Italian-American anarchist convicted and executed (along with Nicola Sacco) for murder in a highly publicized and controversial trial, now widely believed to have been innocent of the crimes for which Sacco and Vanzetti were executed. *(1888)*

Government and Military

Charles Rangel, long-time member of the US House of Representatives, first African-American to chair the House Ways and Means Committee, helped found the Congressional Black Caucus. *(1930)*

Joseph Warren, American physician and patriot in the American Revolution, best known for enlisting Paul Revere and William Dawes to spread the alarm about British troop movements prior to the Battles of Lexington and Concord. *(1741)*

Literature and Journalism

Robert Munsch, wrote the famous children's book *Love You Forever. (1945)*

Athol Fugard, South African playwright and novelist best known for the 1982 drama *"Master Harold"...and the Boys*, and for the novel *Tsotsi*, adapted into an Academy Award-winning film in 2006. *(1932)*

William Styron, novelist best known for *Sophie's Choice* and *The Confessions of Nat Turner. (1925)*

Yasunari Kawabata (川端 康成**),** novelist and short story writer who won the 1968 Nobel Prize in Literature, the first Japanese author to receive that honor. *(1899)*

Joseph Warren, by John Singleton Copley

Jeannette Rankin (Courtesy Library of Congress)

Ben Jonson, English playwright and poet, considered second only to Shakespeare in Jacobean England, best known works include *Volpone* and *The Alchemist. (1572*)*

Music

Graham Russell, singer and guitarist for Air Supply. *(1950)*

Frank Beard, drummer for the rock band ZZ Top. *(1949)*

Carmine Coppola, composed the soundtracks to the *Godfather* films, directed by his son Francis Ford Coppola. *(1910)*

Richard Strauss, German composer of operas and other instrumental works, including *Also sprach Zarathustra* (best known for its use in the 1968 film *2001: A Space Odyssey*), and the opera *Der Rosenkavalier. (1864)*

Notable Women

Jeannette Rankin, first woman to hold federal office in the United States, elected from Montana in 1916 to become a member of the US House of Representatives. *(1880)*

---

* Exact date uncertain, but most sources list June 11.

Millicent Fawcett, intellectual and political leader known for her advocacy of women's right to vote. *(1847)*

Lucy Pickens, socialite known as the "Queen of the Confederacy" who became the stereotype of the "Southern belle," later the only woman to be depicted on Confederate currency. *(1832)*

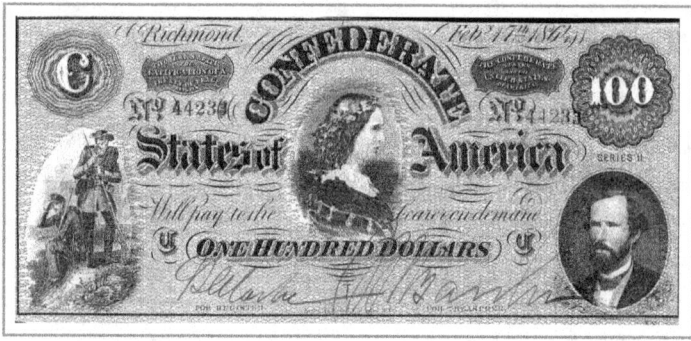

Confederate $100 bill featuring Lucy Pickens

Anne Neville, wife of English monarch Richard III, who appears as a character in Shakespeare's play of the same name. *(1456)*

Performing Arts

Shia LaBeouf, actor whose best known films are *Transformers* (and sequels) and *Indiana Jones and the Kingdom of the Crystal Skull. (1986)*

Joshua Jackson, actor known for playing Pacey in *Dawson's Creek,* Charlie in *The Mighty Ducks* film series, and Peter Bishop in *Fringe. (1978)*

Peter Dinklage, actor best known for playing Tyrion Lannister in the HBO series *Game of Thrones,* which which he won two Emmys and a Golden Globe Award. *(1969)*

Hugh Laurie, actor best known for playing the title character in the TV series *House,* and previously for his partnership with Stephen Fry in *Jeeves and Wooster. (1959)*

Adrienne Barbeau, actress best known for playing the daughter in the sitcom *Maude,* and for sex symbol roles in such films as Creepshow and *Swamp Thing. (1945)*

Chad Everett, actor best known for playing Dr. Joe Gannon in the 1970s TV series *Medical Center. (1937)*

Gene Wilder, comic actor best known for such films as *The Producers, Blazing Saddles, Young Frankenstein,* and *Willy Wonka & the Chocolate Factory. (1933)*

Michael Cacoyannis (Μιχάλης Κακογιάννης), film director best known for the 1964 film *Zorba the Greek,* which received three Academy Award nominations. *(1921)*

Hazel Scott, actress, pianist, and singer, host of *The Hazel Scott Show* (1950), the first television show hosted by a person of color. *(1920) (Photo next page.)*

Magda Gabor, actress and socialite, elder siste of Zsa Zsa and Eva Gabor. *(1915)*

Hazel Scott in *Rhapsody in Blue* (1945)

Science and Technology

Mehmet Oz, physician and host of *The Dr. Oz Show. (1960)*

Robin Warren, Australian pathologist who shared the 2005 Nobel Prize in Physiology or Medicine for proving that the *H. pylori* bacterium was the infectious cause of stomach ulcers, and for developing a convenient diagnostic test for it.*(1937)*

Jacques-Yves Cousteau, French oceanographer, conservationist, and documentary filmmaker known for his award-winning films on undersea discovery; invented the aqualung. *(1910)*

Jacques-Yves Cousteau (Photo: Hans Peters, Anefo)

Carl von Linde, German engineer who developed industrial-scale air separation and gas liquefication processes, and discovered the refrigeration cycle, received the 1913 Nobel Prize in Physics. *(1842)*

Sports

José Reyes, New York Mets' all-time leader in triples and stolen bases. *(1983)*

Diana Taurasi, basketball player who is one of only 9 women to win an Olympic gold medal, and NCAA championship, and a WNBA championship. *(1982)*

Geoff Ogilvy, golfer who won the 2006 US Open and three World Golf Championships. *(1977)*

Sandra Schmirler, led the Canadian curling team to a gold medal at the 1998 Winter Olympics; member of the Canadian Sports Hall of Fame and the World Curling Federation Hall of Fame. *(1963)*

Joe Montana, football quarterback primarily for the San Francisco 49ers, first player ever named Super Bowl MVP three times, elected to the Pro Football Hall of Fame in his first year of eligibility. *(1956)*

Jackie Stewart, Formula One racing driver nicknamed the "Flying Scot," considered among the greatest Formula One drivers of all time, later a sports announcer for ABC. *(1939)*

Vince Lombardi, best known as head coach of the Green Bay Packers, leading them to five NFL championships and victory in the first two Super Bowls; namesake of the NFL Super Bowl Trophy; member of the Pro Football Hall of Fame. *(1913)*

Ernie Nevers *(right),* multi-sport athlete who played football for Duluth and Chicago and baseball for St. Louis, named to the College Football Hall of Fame and the Pro Football Hall of Fame; remains the only NFL player in history to score 40 points in a single game. *(1903)*

Cap Fear, football player with the Toronto Argonauts inducted into both the Canadian Football Hall of Fame and the Canada's Sports Hall of Fame. *(1901)*

Hugo Wieslander, Swedish athlete awarded the 1912 Olympic Gold medal in the decathalon after the fact, when original winner Jim Thorpe was disqualified for not being an amateur when it was discovered he had played professional baseball for a minor league team. In 1982, Thorpe was reinstated as joint winner with Wieslander. *(1889)*

Roger Bresnahan, baseball player and manager nicknamed "the Duke of Tralee," named in 1945 to the Baseball Hall of Fame. *(1879)*

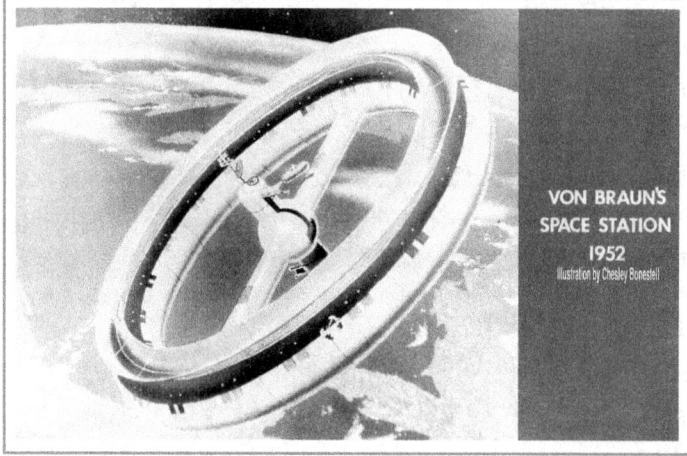

1952 space station concept deeloped by Dr. Wernher von Braun,
ilustrated by Chesley Bonestell (Courtesy NASA)

Who Died on June 11?

Art and Illustration

Chesley Bonestell, painter whose realistic astronomical paintings helped inspire the American space program, also did paintings and special effects for such films as *Citizen Kane. (1986)*

Business

Robert Fogel, economic historian who shared the 1993 Nobel Memorial Prize in Economic Sciences for his work in applying economic theory to explain institutional change. *(2013)*

Eilyahu M. Goldratt, management theorist who developed management tools and processes in industrial and project management, wrote the 1984 best-selling "management novel" *The Goal.* (2011)

Egon von Fürstenberg, prince and fashion / interior designer known for his partnership with spouse Diane von Fürstenberg. *(2004)*

Samuel Whitbread, brewer who founded Whitbread & Company, which became one of the largest beer producers in Great Britain. *(1796)*

Crime and Punishment

Timothy McVeigh, American domestic terrorist
convicted and executed for the 1995 Oklahoma City
bombing in 1995, which killed 168 and injured over
600. *(2001)*

Government and Politics

Thích Quảng Đức, Vietnamese Buddhist monk
famous for his self-immolation in Saigon as a
political protest, resulting in a photograph by
Malcolm Browne that was named World Press Photo
of the Year and led to and the eventual toppling of
the Diệm government. *(1963)*

The famous photograph of the self-immolation of Thích Quảng Đức
by Malcolm Browne for the Associated Press (© AP)

Klemens von Metternich, Austrian nobleman and diplomat who served as foreign minister and chancellor of the Austrian Empire. *(1859)*

Klemens von Metternich, by Thomas Lawrence

George I, German nobleman who became king of Great Britain and Ireland as the first monarch of the House of Hanover. While there were more than 50 people with closer blood ties to the monarchy, they were Roman Catholics and forbidden from inheriting the throne; George I was the closest relative who was a Protestant. *(1727)*

Literature and Journalism

David Brinkley, newscaster and journalist who co-hosted *The Huntley-Brinkley Report, NBC Nightly News,* and *This Week with David Brinkley;* member of the Television Hall of Fame and recipient of the Presidential Medal of Freedom. *(2003)*

Catherine Cookson, English author whose books sold more than 100 million copies, at one time the most widely read novelist in the United Kingdom. *(1998)*

Robert E. Howard, American pulp fiction writer best known for his stories featuring the character *Conan the Barbarian. (1936)*

Military and Adventure

Daniel Carter Beard, youth leader whose "Sons of Daniel Boone" organization was merged with the Boy Scouts of America when it was first formed in 1910; founded Boy Scouts Troop 1. *(1941)*

David Brinkley

Ornette Coleman (Photo: Michael Hoefner, CC BY-SA 3.0)

Sir John Franklin, British naval officer and Arctic explorer, whose last expedition, an attempt to chart and navigate the Northwest Passage ended with the death of his entire crew. *(1847)*

Music

Ornette Coleman, jazz saxophonist and trumpeter known as one of the major innovators of the free jazz movement; awarded a MacArthur Fellowship in 1994 and received the 2007 Pulitzer Prize for Music for his album *Sound Grammar;* member of the Down Beat Jazz Hall of Fame. *(2015)*

Performing Arts

Ruby Dee, actress known for such films as *A Raisin in the Sun, The Jackie Robinson Story, Do the Right Thing,* and *American Gangster;* often worked with her husband, actor Ossie Davis. *(2014)*

Ann Rutherford, actress who played Polly in the *Andy Hardy* film series and the sister of Scarlett O'Hara in the 1939 film *Gone With the Wind. (2012)*

DeForest Kelley, actor best known for playing Dr. McCoy on the television and film series *Star Trek.* *(1999) (Photo next page.)*

Brigitte Helm, actress best remembered for playing Maria (human and robot) in the 1927 silent Fritz Lang film *Metropolis. (1996)*

John Wayne, Academy Award winning actor, best known for Westerns, whose many films include *True Grit, Stagecoach, The Man Who Shot Liberty Valance, The Quiet Man, The Longest Day,* and *The Shootist.* (1979) *(Additional photo page 20.)*

John Wayne (left) with Gail Russell in *Angel and the Badman*

Religion

Frank Laubach, missionary known as the "Apostle to the Illiterates" for his literacy efforts that have taught some 60 million people to read in their own language. *(1970)*

Sports

Teófilo Stevenson, Cuban pugilist best known as one of only three boxers ever to win three Olympic gold medals in the sport. *(2012)*

DeForest Kelley as Dr. McCoy on *Star Trek*

Quote of the Day

"Before you say you can't do something, try it."

Kiichiro Toyoda (豊田 喜一郎)
founder of Toyoto Motor Corporation
born June 11 , 1894

Holidays
Around
the World

June 11

King Kamehameha the Great (Courtesy Bishop Museum)

Holidays Around the World

If you're looking for a reason to take your special day off, you should know that every single day is a holiday somewhere in the world! Here's some of what you can celebrate on June 11!

Data Magna da Marinha do Brasil
Brazilian Navy Commemorative Day celebrates the achievements and service of the navy of Brazil on June 11.

Davis Day (William Davis Miners' Memorial Day)
Coal mining communities in **Nova Scotia, Canada,** observes an annual day of remembrance on June 11 for miners killed on the job in that province.

Kamehameha Day
Hawaii honors Kamehameha the Great with a public holiday on June 11. King Kamehameha first unified the islands in the 18th century.

Student's Day
Many nations recognize students on a special day. In the **Honduras**, Student's Day is observed on June 11.

Corn on the Cob (Photo: Darwin Bell, CC BY-SA 2.0) — for
NATIONAL CORN ON THE COB DAY

Celebrations About Food

In the United States, almost every day of the year is dedicated to a particular food. (Some other countries also have official food days, but only in America is there one every single day!) Sponsored by manufacturers, retailers, farmers, or simply fans, these days are often proclaimed by the President, Congress, state governors, or mayors. Given that there are more different foods than days of the year, some days honor more than one kind of food!

Some foods just get a day, while others get a whole month. Here's what to eat on June 11 and the rest of the month of June!

Depending where you look, June 11 might be **National Corn on the Cob Day, National German Chocolate Cake Day**, and **National Cotton Candy Day**! We'll happily eat corn on the cob or German chocolate cake any time, and since many fairs take place in June, maybe there'll be a chance for some cotton candy as well!

The whole month of June is set aside to honor the following foods.

- Georgia Blueberry Month
- National Candy Month
- National Dairy Month
- National Fresh Fruit and Vegetables Month
- National Iced Tea Month
- National Papaya Month

Honorary Months

Presidents, Congresses, and nations around the world issue proclamations recognizing particular months to honor certain causes. These events generally fall in April, though honorary months do come and go.

Holidays established by states and nonprofit organizations are listed if verified. If not otherwise specified, all months are US. There is some variation from year to year; some celebratory months get added and others get dropped. Two places to get up to date information are the current edition of Chase's Calendar of Events *or the website Brownielocks. Here are some honorary designations for June.*

- Adopt-a-Cat Month

- African-American Music Appreciation Month

- Bicycle Month (May 25 to June 25) (Canada)
- Caribbean American Heritage Month
- Children's Awareness Month
- Crop over (Barbados), celebrated until the first Monday in August.
- Dairy Alternative Month
- Fireworks Safety Month
- Gay and Lesbian Pride Month (US)
- Great Outdoors Month (US)
- International Surf Music Month
- Men's Health Education and Awareness Month
- National Accordion Awareness Month

Sarah Vaughn, by William P. Gottlieb — for AFRICAN-AMERICAN
MUSIC APPRECIATION MONTH

- National Camping Month
- National Rivers Month
- National Safety Month
- National Smile Month (UK)
- National Oceans Month (United States)
- Season of Emancipation (April 14 to August 23) (Barbados)
- Women's Golf Month
- World Naked Bike Ride Month (northern hemisphere)

Moveable and Multi-Day Events

Some events take place over a specific week or time period. Start and finish dates may vary from year to year. Some events occur on different days each year (such as "fourth Saturday of a month"). These events sometimes take place on June 11.

Second Thursday
- Seersucker Thursday (United States)

A Saturday
- Queen's Official Birthday (United Kingdom) (precise week varies)

Second Saturday
- Start of National Dairy Goat Awareness Week, ending on the third Saturday

HM Queen Elizabeth II inspects the line in the Trooping of the Color, part of the QUEEN'S OFFICIAL BIRTHDAY celebration.

- National Day (Montserrat, Pitcairn Islands, Saint Helena, South Georgia and South Sandwich Islands, Tristan da Cunha (United Kingdom))

Second Sunday

- Canadian Rivers Day
- Children's Day (United States)
- Father's Day (Austria, Belgium)
- Mother's Day (Luxembourg)
- Multicultural American Child Day
- Race Unity Day

Monday before Father's Day in the United States

- International Men's Health Week: (Begins on the Monday before Father's Day, ends on Father's Day (United States)

Monday after the second Saturday

- Queen's Official Birthday (Norfolk Island)

Second Monday

- Queen's Official Birthday (Papua New Guinea, Solomon Islands, Australia, with the exception of Western Australia, which celebrates on the first Monday)
- Singapore International Water Week begins

Just for Fun

Anybody can make up a holiday, and many people do! While none of these are officially recognized and some may come and go, here are a few more holidays for June 11.

- National Making Life Beautiful Day

- World Gin Day

A dry martini (Photo: Hayford Peirce), for WORLD GIN DAY.

Religious Feast Days and Holidays

*Every religion normally has feast days and holidays
associated with it. While some religious days take place on
a given calendar day, others occur on different days each
year, usually because the date is determined by the phases
of the Moon rather than the Earth's path around the Sun.
Here are some religious feasts, festivals, and holidays that
sometimes or always fall on June 11!*

Saint Days

*Each day in the year is considered a feast day for one or
more saints. They are somewhat different in western
Christianity (Catholicism and many forms of
Protestantism) and in eastern (Orthodox) Christianity.*

In **Western Christianity,** June 11 is the feast day
of Saints Barnabas the Apostle and Paula Frassinetti.
The Armenian Catholic Church also honors Blessed
Ignatius Maloyan.

In **Eastern Orthodox Christianity,** it is also the
commemoration of Saints Bartholomew the Apostle
and Barnabas of Vetluga. (These saints are honored
on June 24 by Old Calendrists.†)

In **Coptic Orthodox Christianity,** which uses its
own calendar, June 11 is the equivalent of the 4th day
of the month of Paoni. They commemorate Saints
Sanusi, Amun the Martyr, Sophia, John of Herclea,
Hor, and Pope John VIII of Alexandria.

---

† "Old Calendrists" use the Julian, rather than the Gregorian,
calendar. For an explanation of different calendar types, see "What
Day of the Week is June 11?"

Quote of the Day

"Do you recall that night in June
Upon the Danube River;
We listened to the ländler-tune,
We watched the moonbeams quiver."

— Charles A. Aïdé, "Danube River"

About
the
Month
of

June

June, by Eugène Grasset

June: The Sixth Month

And what is so rare as a day in June?
Then, if ever, come perfect days;
Then Heaven tries earth if it be in tune,
And over it softly her warm ear lays.

— *James Russell Lowell*

In the Julian and Gregorian calendars, June is the sixth month of the year. It's one of the four months that have only 30 days. No months start on the same day of the week as June, an oddity shared only by May. However, June ends on the same day of the week as March in both common and leap years.

In the Northern Hemisphere, June is the month with the longest daylight hours; in the Southern Hemisphere, it's the one with the shortest, equivalent to December. The meteorological summer begins June 21 (the Summer Solstice) in the Northern Hemisphere; the meteorological winter begins on the same day in the Southern Hemisphere (the Winter Solstice).

The English name of June takes its name from the Latin *Iunius*. The poet Ovid gives two theories for the origin of the name. The first is that June is named for the Roman goddess Juno, wife of Jupiter and queen of the gods. The second is that the name comes from the Latin word *iuniores* ("younger ones"), and that the previous month of May comes from *maiores* ("elders")

As the early Roman calendar started its new year in March, June was originally the fourth month of the year. It's uncertain when the Romans switched the new year to January, but it may have been as late as 153 BCE.

June, George Auriol

June in Other Cultures

The month of June has different names in different languages. Some nations use calendars other than the Gregorian, and their months may overlap with June. In lunar-based calendars, such as Islam, months move through the seasons, but they often have a word for June itself.

Albanian: Qershor

Arabic (Egyptian, Sudanese, Moroccan): يونيو
(*yūniyū*)

Arabic (Levantine): حزيران(*ḥuzayrān*)

Arabic (Libyan): الصيف (*al-sayf*)

Arabic (Algerian): جوان (*Juwān*)

Azerbaijani: İyun

Basque: Ekain

Bulgarian: юни (*juni*)

Chinese: 六月 (Cantonese: *luhkyuht*; Mandarin: *liùyuè*; Taiwanese: *lak-goeh*)

Corsican: Chjugnu

Czech: červen

Finnish: Kesäkuu

French: Juin

German, Norwegian: Juni

Greek: Ιούνιος (*Ioúnios*)

Hebrew: יוני (*yûnî*)

Hindi: जून (*jūn*)

Hungarian: Június

Irish (Gaelic): Meitheamh mí an Mheithimh

Italian: Giugno

Japanese (traditional calendar): 六月 (*rokugatsu*); 水無月 (*minaduki*)

Korean: 유월 (*yuweol*)

Lithuanian: Birželis

Maori: Pipiri

Old English: Sēremōnaþ

Polish: Czerwiec

Russian: июнь (*ijun'*)

Sesotho: Phupjane

Spanish: Junio

Swedish, Swahili: Juni

Thai: Mithunayon

Vietnamese: 腩毭 (*tháng sáu*)

Welsh: Mehefin

June Brides (and Other Sayings and Superstitions)

June is the most popular month for weddings, followed by August. There are a number of sayings and superstitions about June brides and June weddings.

> "A June bride is joyful, jubilant, and jolly well jovial."

> "A June bride will be impetuous, and generous."

> "Married in the month of roses (June), life will be one long honeymoon."

> "Marry when June roses grow, over land and sea you'll go."

> "When you marry in June, you'll be a bride all your life." (from the song *June Bride*.)

Which day to get married? That's easy. "Monday for wealth, Tuesday for health, Wednesday the best day of all, Thursday for losses, Friday for crosses, Saturday for no luck at all."

Why such an emphasis on June? Some say it's in honor of Juno, the goddess of marriage. Others suggest it's because back in Medieval days, people would usually have their (yes) annual bath in May, so they'd still be relatively fresh by June. This may also explain the custom of the bridal bouquet.

According to superstition, May is the most unlucky month for marriages, but in ancient Rome the "inauspicious" period ran from May 15 to June 15. The high priestess of Jupiter told the poet Ovid to delay his daughter's wedding until after that date.

There are also some June proverbs for farmers.

"A calm June puts the farmer in tune."

"June damp and warm, does the farmer no harm."

June Symbols

Birthstone Pearl, moonstone, or alexandrite.

Pearl

Moonstone

Alexandrite

Birth Flowers Rose and Honeysuckle

Roses, by Vincent van Gogh

Honeysuckle

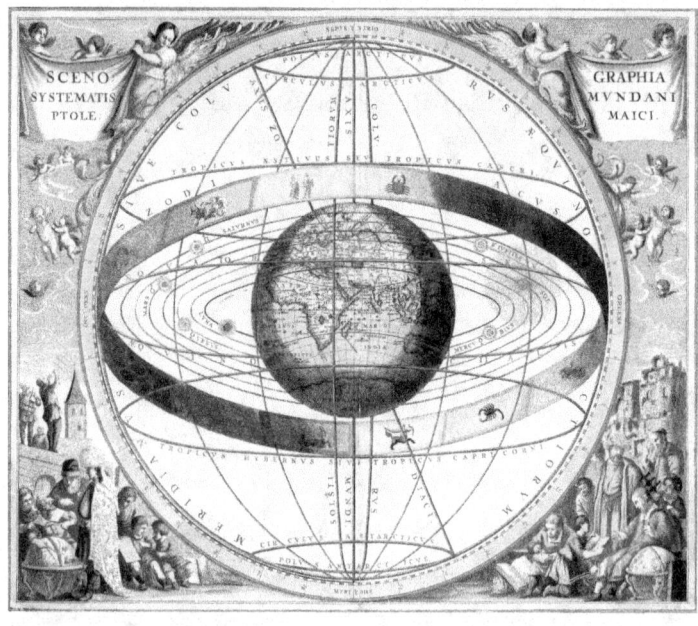

Scenography of the Ptolemaic Cosmography, by Johannes van Loon, based on Andreas Cellarius's *Harmonia Macrocosmica*, 1660

June 11 Zodiac Signs

From the perspective of someone on Earth, the Sun appears to move through the sky throughout the year, along a path astronomers call the *ecliptic plane*. The ecliptic plane is divided into twelve constellations, known as the zodiac, based on traditionally observed patterns of stars. On your birthday, you can't see your constellation, because it's in the daytime sky.

The zodiac was first developed by Babylonian astronomers about 2,500 years ago. Because they were unaware that the Earth wobbles like a spinning top (known as *precession*), they didn't make allowance for the fact that the Sun's path through the zodiac changes over time.

That means there are now two sets of dates for your birth sign. The *tropical dates* are the original Babylonian dates; the *sidereal dates* tell you where the Sun actually appears as it moves along its annual path.

For June 11, the tropical sign is **Gemini** and the sidereal sign is **Taurus.**

Taurus

Tropical April 21 to May 22
Siderial May 16 to June 15

In Greek mythology, Taurus was a disguise adopted by Zeus, who appeared to the maiden Europa in the form of a gentle white bull. Europa unwisely got too close, and Zeus kidnapped her to the island of Crete, where she bore him three sons, including Minos, builder of the labyrinth that housed the minotaur.

In astrology, Taurus is an earth sign, and Taureans are supposed to be quiet, gentle, compassionate, and stubborn. Taureans can appreciate the finer things in life and are cautious with money.

Gemini

Tropical May 22 to June 21
Sidereal June 16 to July 15

According to Greek mythology, Leda, wife of the King of Sparta, gave birth to Helen of Troy and Clytemnestra. The god Zeus, disguised as a swan, seduced her after she had already lain with her husband on the same night. This resulted in two eggs, which hatched to become the twins Castor and Pollux. Castor's father was the King of Sparta, but Pollux was the son of Zeus and therefore immortal. When Castor died, Pollux shared his immortality, so that they could divide their time between Hades and Olympus. They were enshrined in the Zodiac as the constellation Gemini, the Twins.

In astrology, Gemini is an air sign, ruled by Mercury, compatible with Libra, Aquarius, and Aries. Geminis are supposed to be communicative, flexible, intellectual, and curious, but prone to fickleness and easily distracted.

Illustration by Edward Penfield

What Day of the Week is June 11?

On what day of the week does June 11 fall?

Surprisingly, this isn't an easy question. Because the calendar year is 365 days long (366 in leap years), it doesn't divide evenly by the seven days of the week.

Also, the Earth goes around the Sun in about 365-1/4 days, so a calendar tends to drift over time. That's why the same date falls on different weekdays in different years.

This is made even more complicated by a change in calendars that took place in 1582. Our modern calendar has its roots in ancient Rome, in a calendar reform conducted by Julius Caesar. Caesar commissioned mathematicians to attack the problem, and they came up with the idea of leap years, and thus standardized the calendar for centuries to come. This was called the Julian calendar.

Over time, however, the small errors in Caesar's calculation compounded. That's why Pope Gregory XIII commissioned the Gregorian calendar, used in most of the world today. Some countries converted in 1582, when the calendar was first developed; some converted later; other still haven't changed.

Gregorian and Julian aren't the only types of calendars. The Hebrew year, the Islamic year, and many other calendars are used in different parts of the world and among different people.

You can convert Gregorian dates to other calendars, including the Hebrew calendar, the Islamic calendar, and even the Mayan calendar by visiting the Fourmilab Calendar Converter at http://www.fourmilab.ch/documents/calendar/.

Chinese calendar systems are quite complex and have changed several times; a full discussion is far beyond the scope of this book. If you're interested, you can find information here: http://www.hermetic.ch/cal_stud/chinese_cal.htm.

On Names and Dates

Historians use "CE" (Common Era) and "BCE" (Before the Common Era) instead of the more common "AD" (Anno Domini, or Year of Our Lord) and "BC" (Before Christ), reflecting the fact that the year-numbering system established by the Gregorian calendar is used throughout the world in many countries not culturally Christian.

The CE/BCE designation dates back to at least 1708, and has been adopted as a standard by the United Nations and the Universal Postal Union. Because this series of books covers events and people of all nations and cultures, we use the CE/BCE terms.

The abbreviation "O.S." ("Old Style") and "N.S." ("New Style") on some dates refers to the fact that the Russian Empire (in particular) did not switch from the Julian to the Gregorian calendar at the same time as the rest of Europe, and therefore some figures and events have two dates.

Also, in the Julian calendar in England in the 16th century, the year began on March 25 rather than January 1. To avoid confusion with Gregorian dates, dates between January and March were often written using both years.

People and events whose original names are not in the Western alphabet have their native names (where possible) in the appropriate script shown in parenthesis. If you are using an e-reader to access an electronic version of this book, all characters don't always display on all devices.

A 50-year brass perpetual calendar.

Quote of the Day

"Time is an illusion, lunchtime doubly so."

Douglas Adams,
from *The Hitchhiker's Guide to the Galaxy*

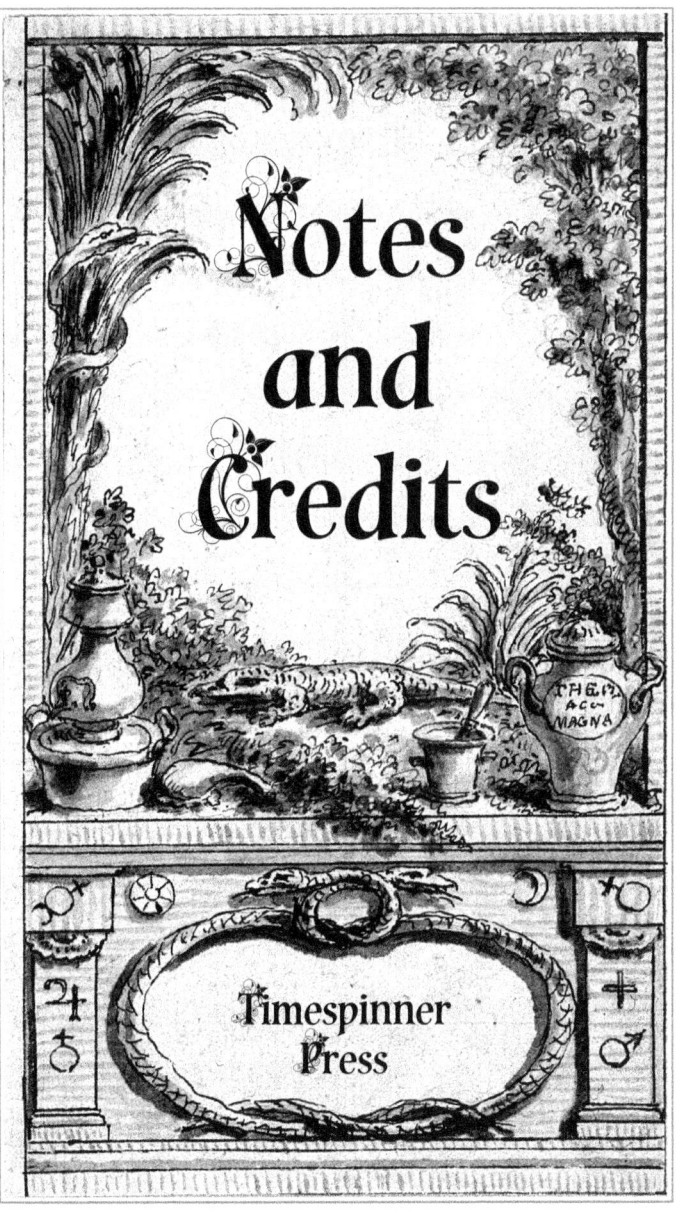

Notes and Credits

Timespinner
Press

Cartoon by John T. McCutcheon

Copyright, Credit, and Contact

Follow Us

Our blog "This Day in History" (http://
timespinnerpress.com/this-day-in-history/) features short
articles on events and people associated with each day, and
updates several times each week. Also subscribe to the
"Quote of the Day" at http://timespinnerpress.com/quote-
of-the-day/. You can get daily links by following us on
Facebook at TimespinnerPress, or on Twitter as
@sidewisethinker.

Contact Us

Find an error or a format problem? Want information about
the series, about us, or about when the volume for your
special day might be available? Please email us at
editor@timespinnerpress.com. (We also take requests if your
special day isn't yet complete. Please give us at least six
weeks' notice if possible.)

Sources

We owe a great debt to Wikipedia, which is our first stop for
research. We attempt to make independent confirmation of
all important dates and facts through a variety of other
sources.

Other sources we frequently use include the Library of
Congress; "on this day" listings from *Encyclopedia Britannica*,
the *New York Times*, and the BBC; Omniglot for the names of
months in other languages; *Chase's Calendar of Events*; and, of
course, the always essential Google.

All art and photographs are either in the public domain, used under a Creative Commons license, or with a "fair use" justification, and most frequently come from Wikimedia Commons and the Library of Congress Prints and Photographs Division.

Attribution is provided where possible, or as requested by the copyright owner, or when there is particular historical significance, listed below. For information about any particular illustration or photograph, please contact us.

Credits

1. The cover photograph is from John Trumbull's 1819 painting *Declaration of Independence,* which can be found on the back of the US $2 bill and (in the original) in the US Capitol rotunda. The painting is in the public domain because its copyright has expired; the photograph of the painting is in the public domain both because it is a faithful reproduction of a two-dimensional public domain work of art, and because it was taken by an employee of the Architect of the Capitol as part of that person's official duties.

2. The illustration of the month of June used on the back cover is from the French Gothic illuminated manuscript *Les Très Riches Heures du duc de Berry* by the Limbourg Brothers, Jean Colombe, and an intermediate painter whose name is lost to history. It is in the public domain because its copyright has expired.

3. The box graphic used on the first page is from a 1916 pamphlet entitled "Divorce versus Democracy" authored by G. K. Chesterton, originally published in London by the Society of St. Peter and St. Paul. It is in the public domain in the US because it was published prior to 1923, and is in the public domain in all countries (including the country of origin) in which the copyright time is the author's life plus 70 years or less.

4. The graphic design for the section pages in this book is from a design originally created for a pharmacy label. It is

courtesy of Wellcome Images (ICV No 11073, photo V0010813), and is used here under CC BY-SA 4.0.

5. The detail of the Committee of Five is cropped from the same John Trumbull painting on the cover. (See #1, above.)

6. The handwritten draft of the Declaration of Independence is from the collections of the Library of Congress. It is in the public domain because its copyright has expired.

7. The painting *Writing the Declaration of Independence* by Jean Leon Gerome Ferris is from the collection of the Virginia Historical Society. It is in the public domain because its copyright has expired. The image is from the Library of Congres, digital ID cph.3g09904.

8. The front page of the July 6, 1776, issue of the *Pennsylvania Evening Post* is in the public domain because its copyright has expired. The image is courtesy of the American Revolution Center.

9. The 1962 FBI photograph of dummy heads used in the escape from Alcatraz is in the public domain as a work created by an employee of the US government as part of that person's official duties.

10. The 1895 photograph of Émile Levassor and Charles d'Hostingue is in the public domain because its copyright has expired.

11. The 1934 poster from the film *Blue Steel* is in the public domain because it was published in the United States between 1923 and 1977 without a copyright notice.

12. The 1802 painting *Dedham Vale* by John Constable is in the public domain because its copyright has expired. The original is in the collection of the Victoria and Albert Museum, London, accession number 124-1888.

13. The circa 1765 painting *Portrait of Joseph Warren* by John Singleton Copley is in the public domain because its copyright has expired. The original is in the collection of the Museum of Fine Arts, Boston, accession number 95.1366.

14. The 1917 photograph of Jeannette Rankin is from the Library of Congress, digital ID cph.3b13863. It is in the public domain because its copyright has expired.

15. The Confederate $100 bill is not an object of copyright, and
    in any event was published before 1923, so is in the public
    domain.

16. The 1945 screenshot from the trailer of the film *Rhapsody in
    Blue* is in the public domain because it was published in the
    United States between 1923 and 1977 without a copyright
    notice. Traditionally, film trailers are not copyrighted
    because of the way in which they are intended to be used.

17. The 1972 photograph of Jacques-Yves Cousteau is by Hans
    Peters for Anefo, and is used here under CC BY-SA 3.0.

18. The Underwood & Underwood photograph of Ernie Nevers
    was published prior to January 1, 1923, and is therefore in
    the public domain.

19. The cover from the 1952 space station concept is in the
    public domain as a work created solely by NASA (MSFC
    Reference Number MSFC-75-SA-4105-2C).

20. The 1963 World Press Photo of the Year of the self-
    immolation of Thích Quảng Đức by Malcome Browne was
    taken for the Associated Press, and is presumed to be
    copyrighted either by Browne or the AP. Its use here is
    under "fair use" provisions of copyright law. It illustrates a
    story about the photograph itself, there is no free media
    equivalent, and it is important to the understanding of the
    historical event in question. It is unlikely to replace or limit
    the original market role of the copyrighted media as it is
    printed in a small size and lowresolution unsuitable for the
    production of counterfeit works. No challenge to the
    copyright status of the original work is intended.

21. The 1815 portrait of Klemens von Metternich by Thomas
    Lawrence is in the public domain because its copyright has
    expired. It is from the collection of the Kunshistorisches
    Museum, Vienna.

22. The 1962 NBC News publicity photograph of David Brinkley
    is in the public domain because it was published in the
    United States between 1923 and 1977 without a copyright
    notice. Traditionally, publicity photographs are not
    copyrighted because of the way in which they are intended
    to be used.

23. The 2011 photograph of Ornette Coleman is by Michael Hoefner and is used here under CC BY-SA 3.0.

24. The 1947 publicity photograph from the film *Angel and the Badman* is in the public domain because it was published in the United States between 1923 and 1977 without a copyright notice. Traditionally, publicity photographs are not copyrighted because of the way in which they are intended to be used.

25. The 1970 publicity photograph of DeForest Kelley from *Star Trek* is in the public domain because it was published in the United States between 1923 and 1977 without a copyright notice. Traditionally, publicity photographs are not copyrighted because of the way in which they are intended to be used.

26. The artist who painted the portrait of King Kamehameha is unknown. The original is in the collection of the Bishop Museum, Honolulu.

27. The 2006 photograph of corn on the cob is by Darwin Bell, and is used here under CC BY-SA 2.0.

28. The 1946 photograph of Sarah Vaughn was taken by William P. Gottlieb, and is part of the William P. Gottlieb Collection of jazz photographs at the Library of Congress. In accordance with the wishes of Gottlieb, the photographs in the collection entered into the public domain in 2010.

29. The 2008 photograph of the Trooping of the Color was taken by "Ibagli," who released the work into the public domain without restrictions.

30. The 2006 photograph of a martini was taken by Hayford Peirce, who released the work into the public domain without restrictions.

31. The 1896 drawing "June" by Eugène Grasset is in the public domain because its copyright has expired.

32. The 1912 graphic of June by George Auriol is in the public domain because its copyright has expired.

33. The 1815 woodcut of a proposal is in the public domain because its copyright has expired.

34. The photo of a pearl necklace is by "Anna reg," taken from Wikimedia Commons and used here under CC BY-SA 3.0.

35. The photograph of a Brazilian moonstone is by Didier Descouens, taken from Wikimedia Commons and used here under CC BY-SA 4.0.

36. The photograph of alexandrite under ultraviolet light is by Parent Géry, taken from Wikimedia Commons and used here because the creator has dedicated the rights to the public domain under CC0 1.0.

37. The painting *Roses* by Vincent Van Gogh can be found in the collection of the National Gallery of Art, Washington, DC. The image is in the public domain because its copyright has expired.

38. The illustration of honeysuckle originally appeared in the book *American Homes and Gardens*, published by Munn & Co., New York, in 1905. It is in the public domain because its copyright has expired. The image was taken from Flickr's The Commons.

39. The celestial sphere is from *Scenography of the Ptolemaic Cosmography*, by Johannes van Loon, based on Andreas Cellarius's *Harmonia Macrocosmica*, 1660. It is in the public domain because its copyright has expired.

40. The 1906 automobile calendar is by Edward Penfield, and is in the collection of the Library of Congress Prints and Photographs Division. It is in the public domain because its copyright has expired.

41. The 50-year perpetual calendar photograph is in the public domain.

42. The painting "June" is from the *Brevarium Grimani*, circa 1510, and is in the public domain because its copyright has expired.

License Description and Terms

Aside from material purely in the public domain, photographs and other material in this book are used under specific licenses permitting free use, usually with an attribution requirement. For full text and terms of these licenses, click or enter the appropriate links below. If you believe there is an error in the copyright status or attribution of any of these images, please email us.

- Creative Commons Attribution 2.0 Generic (CC-BY 2.0): http://creativecommons.org/licenses/by/2.0/deed.en
- Creative Commons Attribution-Share Alike 3.0 Generic (CC-BY-SA 3.0): http://creativecommons.org/licenses/by-sa/3.0/
- Creative Commons Attribution-Share Alike 2.5 Generic (CC-BY-SA 2.5): http://creativecommons.org/licenses/by-sa/2.5/deed.en
- Creative Commons Attribution-Share Alike 2.0 Generic (CC-BY-SA 2.0): http://creativecommons.org/licenses/by/2.0/deed.en
- Creative Commons Attribution-Share Alike 1.0 Generic (CC-BY-SA 1.0): http://creativecommons.org/licenses/by-sa/1.0/deed.en
- CC0 1.0 Universal (CC0 1.0) Public Domain Dedication (CC0 1.0) http://creativecommons.org/publicdomain/zero/1.0/deed.en
- GNU Free Documentation License (GFDL): http://en.wikipedia.org/wiki/Wikipedia:Text_of_the_GNU_Free_Documentation_License
- License Art Libre (Free Art License): http://artlibre.org

Timespinner
Press

"June," from the *Brevarium Grimani* by Simon Bening (c.1510)

Other Books from Timespinner Press

The Story of a Special Day
Michael Dobson

A series of (eventually) 366 volumes covering everything that happened on your special day! Events, births, deaths, quotes, holidays, and much more. It's like a birthday card they'll never throw away!

US$7.95 print / US$2.99 ebook.

From Plassey to Pakistan
Humayun Mirza

The history of British Colonial India and the formation of Pakistan from the unique perspective of the son of Pakistan's first president and last of the royal line of Bengal, Bihar, and Orissa! This unique historical document tells the inside story of this distinguished family, including the detailed story of the coup that toppled his father from power!

US$27.95 print

A Whole New Navy: America's War in the Pacific

Miles Durr

The most comprehensive and detailed description of America's naval war in the Pacific ever—every battle, every ship, every task force and every task group from Pearl Harbor through the Japanese surrender! A must-have for the collection of every World War II buff!

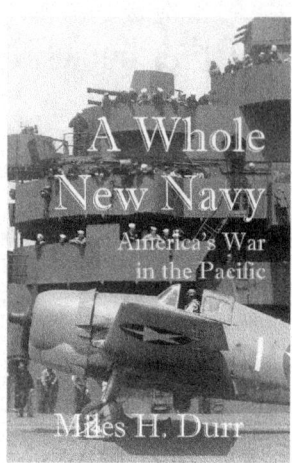

US$29.95 print

Improbable History: The Weird, the Obscure, and the Strangely Important

edited by Michael Dobson

From the birth of Western civilization to the rescue of Apollo 13, from the Leaning Tower of Pisa to Florence's Duomo, history has often turned on small, improbable details. Whatever happened to the ancient Samaritan people? Why did a fortuitous rainstorm allow the British to conquer India? How did an air raid in Italy lead to the development of chemotherapy? What happened when Albert Einstein met Adolf Hitler on the streets of Berlin? How did the Japanese manage to attack the US mainland using balloons? A cast of award-winning writers tackle some of the strangest tales in history!

US$19.95 print